P9-DJV-567

Math Lesson Starters

for the Common Core
Grades 6–8

Other Eye On Education Books Available from Routledge
(www.routledge.com/eyeoneducation)

Guided Math in Action: Building Each Student's Mathematical Proficiency with Small–Group Instruction
Nicki Newton

Using Children's Literature to Teach Problem Solving in Math: Addressing the Common Core in K–2
Jeanne White

Strategies for Common Core Mathematics: Implementing the Standards for Mathematical Practice
Leslie Texas and Tammy Jones

Rigor Is Not a Four-Letter Word
Barbara R. Blackburn

Rigor in Your Classroom: A Toolkit for Teachers
Barbara R. Blackburn

Common Core Literacy Lesson Plans: Ready-to-Use Resources, 6–8
Lauren Davis

Math in Plain English: Literacy Strategies for the Mathematics Classroom
Amy Benjamin

RTI in Math: Evidence-Based Interventions for Struggling Students
Linda Forbringer and Wendy Fuchs

Family Math Night: Middle School Math Standards in Action
Jennifer Taylor-Cox and Christine Oberdorf

Using Formative Assessment to Drive Mathematics Instruction, Grades 3–5
Christine Oberdorf and Jennifer Taylor-Cox

Solving Behavior Problems in Math Class: Academic Learning, Social, and Emotional Empowerment (Grades K–12)
Jennifer Taylor-Cox

RTI Strategies That Work in the 3–6 Classroom
Eli Johnson and Michelle Karns

Assessing Critical Thinking in Middle and High Schools: Meeting the Common Core
Rebecca Stobaugh

Math Lesson Starters

for the Common Core
Grades 6–8

Activities Aligned to the Standards and Assessments

Paige Graiser, Ed.D.

Routledge
Taylor & Francis Group

NEW YORK AND LONDON

First published 2014
by Routledge
711 Third Avenue, New York, NY 10017

and by Routledge
2 Park Square, Milton Park, Abingdon, Oxon OX14 4RN

Routledge is an imprint of the Taylor & Francis Group, an informa business

© 2014 Taylor & Francis

The right of the Author to be identified as author of this work has been asserted by her in accordance with sections 77 and 78 of the Copyright, Designs and Patents Act 1988.

All rights reserved. The purchase of this copyright material confers the right on the purchasing institution to photocopy pages which bear the photocopy icon and copyright line at the bottom of the page. No other part of this publication may be reproduced, stored in a retrieval system, or transmitted in any form or by any means, electronic, mechanical, photocopying, recording or otherwise, without prior permission in writing from the publisher.

Trademark notice: Product or corporate names may be trademarks or registered trademarks, and are used only for identification and explanation without intent to infringe.

Library of Congress Cataloging-in-Publication Data

Graiser, Paige, author.
    Math lesson starters for the common core, grades 6–8 : activities aligned to the standards and assessments / by Paige Graiser.
        pages cm
    Includes index.
    1. Mathematics—Study and teaching (Middle school)—Activity programs—United States.   2. Mathematics—Study and teaching (Middle school)—Standards—United States.   I. Title.
    QA13.G73   2014
    510.71'2—dc23
    2013048655

ISBN: 978-1-138-02323-9 (hbk)
ISBN: 978-1-138-02324-6 (pbk)
ISBN: 978-1-315-77659-0 (ebk)

Typeset in Times New Roman
by Apex CoVantage, LLC

In mathematics the art of proposing a question must be held of higher value than solving it.

George Cantor

Contents

Acknowledgments

This book would not have been possible without the love and support of my husband, Richard; my mother, Nancy; and my children, Elizabeth and Alex. I would also like to thank Lauren for guiding me through the publishing process.

Meet the Author

Dr. Paige Graiser has taught elementary, middle, and high school mathematics in both private and public schools and worked as a Mathematics Consultant with the Southern Regional Education Board (SREB) in Atlanta, Georgia. She earned her Ed.D. from Nova Southeastern University in Ft. Lauderdale, Florida, and is currently a contracted mathematics consultant. She also regularly presents mathematics workshops for schools and districts and is frequently an invited presenter for state and national conferences.

Dr. Graiser has experience working with K–12 math teachers, providing staff development in the areas of implementing the CCSS-M, reading and writing in mathematics, designing effective mathematics lessons, and engaging students in mathematics. She is also a trainer for the Mathematics Design Collaborative (MDC), a Bill and Melinda Gates Foundation initiative. Paige is married to Richard, a middle-grades teacher, and they are the proud parents of Elizabeth and Alex.

Lesson Starters, the Common Core State Standards for Mathematics, and This Book

To truly master the Common Core State Standards for Mathematics (CCSS-M), students will need multiple opportunities to practice concepts throughout the school year. Gone are the days when students learned about a concept during a chapter of instruction and then forgot about the topic until it was time to cram for the state assessment. And, speaking of assessments, those are changing, too. With the implementation of the CCSS-M, there will also be new versions of end-of-year assessments that are being developed by two consortia, Smarter Balanced Assessment Consortium (referred to as Smarter Balanced) and Partnership for Assessment of Readiness for College and Careers (PARCC).

These new assessments are moving away from the old bubble/fill-in-the-blank tests where students had a 25 percent chance of guessing a correct answer. These new assessments will require students to demonstrate and apply their knowledge in a variety of ways such as short answer questions, extended response questions, and performance tasks. There will still be some multiple-choice questions, but these too have been retooled and will provide both teachers and parents with better information on how well students have mastered the standards and will pinpoint the areas in which individual students need additional support.

This book is designed to provide middle-grades math teachers with daily Lesson Starters that not only meet the CCSS-M but also engage students in nontraditional questions and problems similar to what they can expect to face as these new assessments are rolled out. Additionally, the Lesson Starters in this book are designed to assist teachers in diagnosing student misconceptions so that daily lessons can be fine-tuned to meet the immediate learning needs of their students.

What Is a Lesson Starter, and How Can It Improve Classroom Instruction and Behavior Management?

Lesson Starters, often known to teachers and students as *warm-ups*, *bellringers*, or *do-nows*, provide an opportunity for students to ease into the lesson of the day. In addition to being an academic activity that focuses students on the lesson that is about to begin, Lesson Starters are also a valuable behavior management tool. During the first three to five minutes of class (and even as students are entering the classroom before the bell rings), teachers are often bombarded with calls from the office, late students, notes that need to be signed, and myriad other interruptions. During this time, teachers are also expected to complete administrative activities such as performing change-of-class hall duty and taking attendance. These activities are more efficiently managed when students have a task to begin as soon as they enter the classroom.

In addition to being a behavior management tool, Lesson Starters also assist teachers in maximizing their valuable instructional time. The behavioral goal of a Lesson Starter is to have every student seated, focused, and working within minutes of entering the classroom. Instructionally, Lesson Starters can accomplish the following:

- Provide students with a "hook" for the day's lesson and engage them in the lesson of the day
- Activate prior knowledge on the objective of the day
- Review previously taught content
- Engage students in self-assessment
- Incorporate literacy strategies into the lesson

Lesson Starters can take many forms. Some teachers have students use notebook paper or index cards for their Lesson Starters. Often teachers have students keep a week's worth of Lesson Starters on one sheet of notebook paper. Other teachers choose to have their students keep their Lesson Starters in their notebooks. Some teachers grade individual Lesson Starters, while others count this activity as a part of a student's class participation. Whichever method a teacher chooses, it does take time for students to settle into the daily Lesson Starter routine.

> What you do the first day of school will determine your success for the rest of the school year. You would not expect a truck driver to haul an expensive load without first making sure he knew how to drive the truck. Neither can you expect students to succeed if they do not know the routines and procedures of your class.
>
> Harry and Rosemary Wong
> *The First Days of School*

Classroom Suggestions for Successful Lesson Starters

1. To maximize class time, make sure that your Lesson Starter is three to five minutes long. Use a timer to make sure that your Lesson Starter does not take up any valuable instructional time.

2. Set aside a place on your whiteboard or use a projector to make sure your Lesson Starter is in the same place every day. Set the expectation for your students that they will enter the classroom quietly and in an orderly manner, take their seats, and begin working on the day's Lesson Starter.

3. Do not use the Lesson Starter as a chance to introduce new material. If a student doesn't understand the question, he or she will not be able to answer it independently. Lesson Starters are an opportune time to review previously taught material.

4. Vary the format of your bell ringers. Try to not use the same type of question or activity over and over again.

5. Save the Lesson Starter in your lesson plan as a reference for next year's activities.

Classroom Expectations
for Lesson Starters

I (the teacher) will . . .	*The students will . . .*
1. . . . provide a meaningful and engaging Lesson Starter each day. It will be posted/displayed in the same place in the classroom each day.	1. . . . enter the classroom quietly and take their seats upon entering the classroom and begin working on the Lesson Starter.
2. . . . make sure that my Lesson Starters provide my students with an opportunity to review previously taught topics, practice basic skills, and build mathematical vocabulary.	2. . . . consider the daily Lesson Starter as a part of the day's lesson and work to the best of their ability until time is called.
3. . . . not let the Lesson Starter become my day's lesson. If students struggle and become discouraged, I will move on with my lesson for the day and promise the students that we will revisit this topic in a future lesson.	3. . . . make notes about questions they want to ask about the content of the Lesson Starter and wait until time is up rather than interrupt the class during this work time.

The Common Core State Standards: Content Standards for Grades 6–8

6	7	8
Ratios and Proportional Relationships		Functions
The Number System		
Equations and Expressions		
Geometry		
Statistics and Probability		

Based on The Common Core State Standards Initiative

The Common Core State Standards: Mathematical Practice Standards for Grades K–12

MP.1. Make sense of problems and persevere in solving them.

MP.2. Reason abstractly and quantitatively.

MP.3. Construct viable arguments and critique the reasoning of others.

MP.4. Model with mathematics.

MP.5. Use appropriate tools strategically.

MP.6. Attend to precision.

MP.7. Look for and make use of structure.

MP.8. Look for and express regularity in repeated reasoning.

Source: The Common Core State Standards Initiative

UNIT 1
CCSS-M Domain RP
Ratios & Proportional Relationships

*Go down deep enough into anything
and you will find mathematics.*

Dean Schlicter

Ratios & Proportional Relationships

In the middle grades, the CCSS domain of Ratios & Proportional Relationships builds upon students' elementary-school math work in measurement, multiplication, and division. Ideally, this domain should be taught within the context of real-world applications. Ratios and proportions are an integral part of daily life and many careers. In the workplace, doctors and nurses determine drug doses on the basis of a patient's weight, while a banker calculates the exchange rate for a foreign currency. At home, ratios and proportional reasoning are involved in everyday activities such as mixing powdered baby formula, calculating a car's MPG, and determining which laundry detergent is the best buy. By providing students with a true understanding of ratios and proportions, we are not only helping our students pass the next test; we are providing them with a critical skill that will make them better consumers and better equipped to take care of themselves and their future families.

Sixth Grade

For grade 6, the concepts included in this domain are designed to expand the types of problems that students can solve by applying multiplication and division. Most of the problem solving at this level centers around rates and ratios, and students will use these concepts to explore simple drawings, find missing values in a table, and convert units of measurement. Students at grade 6 will also model ratios and rates using tables, tape diagrams, and double number lines.

Seventh Grade

For grade 7, students will be asked to apply their knowlege of ratios and rates to solve both one-step and multistep ratio and percent problems involving tax, tips, and percent of increase. Students at grade 7 will also explore problems that include scale drawings, test for equivalent ratios, begin graphing proportional relationships, and explore unit rates as the measure of the steepness of a line (slope).

Eighth Grade

At grade 8, the domain of Ratios and Proportional Relationships is replaced with Functions. In this domain, students will be required to apply their knowledge of ratio, rate, and proportion as they formulate and reason with expressions and equations. Their work will also include modeling with linear equations and solving linear equations as well as systems of linear equations.

Key Vocabulary Terms: Ratios & Proportional Relationships

Sixth Grade	Seventh Grade	Eighth Grade
ratio	proportion	rate of change
unit rate	proportional relationship	bivariate measurement data
percent	constant of proportionality (unit rate)	linear relationship
equivalent ratios	percent of increase	rate of change
tape diagram	percent of decrease	function
double number line diagram	simple interest	
	tax	
	scale drawing	
	proportional relationship	

Vocabulary Notes

_____

_____

_____

_____

_____

_____

_____

_____

Rate Your Knowledge
Proportional Relationships

Think about the terms listed in this chart. Put an X in the boxes that best describe your knowledge of each term.

	I Can Give a Definition	I Can Give an Example	I Have No Idea
Ratio			
Percent			
Unit Rate			
Proportion			
Percent of Increase or Decrease			
Rate of Change			

Teaching Tip

Knowledge rating activities allow students to access and assess their prior knowledge. They are a great strategy to use at the beginning of a new unit of instruction.

Copyright © 2014 Taylor & Francis. Excerpt from *Math Lesson Starters for the Common Core, Grades 6–8: Activities Aligned to the Standards and Assessments* by Paige Graiser, Ed.D.

Ratios and Roses

Twins Jorge and Joel wanted to buy roses for their grandmother.
The local florist was selling a dozen roses for $30.00.

Jorge

This means we can write the ratio **30 : 12** or $2.50 per rose.

Joel

I thought we had to write the ratio the other way, **12 : 30**, or 0.4 roses per dollar.

Can different ratios be written for this situation?
Who is correct in his thinking, Jorge or Joel? Explain.

Copyright © 2014 Taylor & Francis. Excerpt from *Math Lesson Starters for the Common Core, Grades 6–8: Activities Aligned to the Standards and Assessments* by Paige Graiser, Ed.D.

Delores's Ratio Practice

To help her younger sister, Delores, prepare for her test on ratios, Hannah created a practice quiz. Review Delores's answer to Hannah's quiz, and determine which questions Delores answered correctly.

Hannah's Question	Delores's Answer	Is Delores Correct?
Express the following as a ratio: *It rained 5 out of the last 7 days.*	$5 : 7$	☐ Yes ☐ No
Write this ratio as a fraction in lowest terms: *Jayden made 20 out of 24 free throws.*	$\dfrac{10}{12}$	☐ Yes ☐ No
Write this ratio as a fraction in lowest terms: *The ratio of boys to girls was 27 to 15.*	$1\dfrac{4}{5}$	☐ Yes ☐ No
Garden mulch is on sale for $21.50 for 11 pounds. *How much would one pound of garden mulch cost?*	*One pound of garden mulch would cost $1.96.*	☐ Yes ☐ No

For each of the problems missed by Delores, explain what led to her incorrect answer.

Copyright © 2014 Taylor & Francis. Excerpt from *Math Lesson Starters for the Common Core, Grades 6–8: Activities Aligned to the Standards and Assessments* by Paige Graiser, Ed.D.

The Sweet Shop

Cupcakes
5 for $3.00

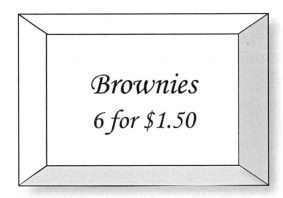

Brownies
6 for $1.50

Courtney wants to buy treats for her friends. If she buys 3 cupcakes and 3 brownies, how much money would she owe?

A. $0.85

B. $1.28

C. $2.55

D. $4.50

How would you explain to Courtney the steps you used to solve this problem?

Copyright © 2014 Taylor & Francis. Excerpt from *Math Lesson Starters for the Common Core, Grades 6–8: Activities Aligned to the Standards and Assessments* by Paige Graiser, Ed.D.

Concrete Proportions

Frank is mixing a small batch of concrete to build a walkway from his driveway to his front porch. He decided to use a 3 : 2 : 1 ratio of sand to gravel to cement. This means that for every three buckets of sand in his mix, Frank will also need two buckets of gravel and one bucket of cement. Frank plans to mix three different batches of concrete for his project.

Using the 3 : 2 : 1 ratio, calculate the missing quantity of materials for each of Frank's batches of concrete.

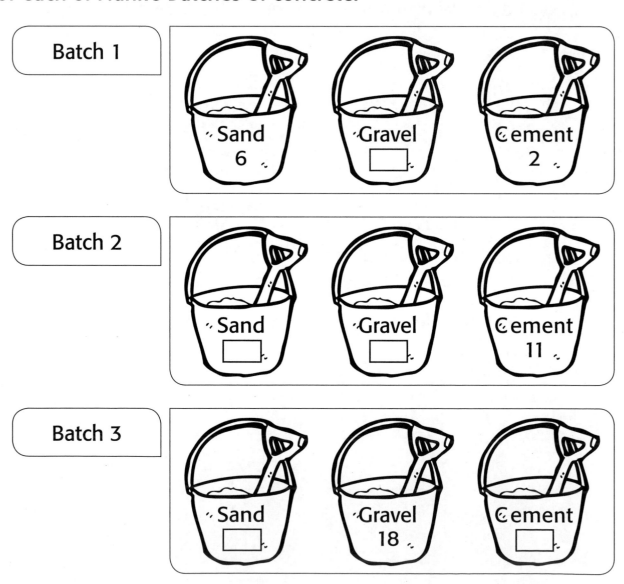

Batch 1

Sand
6

Gravel

Cement
2

Batch 2

Sand

Gravel

Cement
11

Batch 3

Sand

Gravel
18

Cement

Copyright © 2014 Taylor & Francis. Excerpt from *Math Lesson Starters for the Common Core, Grades 6–8: Activities Aligned to the Standards and Assessments* by Paige Graiser, Ed.D.

Interest Fill-In

Fill in the missing words from the sentences below. Use the words provided.

Banks charge their customers a fee for borrowing money. This fee is called _____.

The formula for calculating _____ interest is I = prt.

_____ is the amount of money that is borrowed.

The percentage that is charged is called the _____.

The length of the loan in years is _____.

rate　　simple　　time　　percent

interest　　compound　　principal

Copyright © 2014 Taylor & Francis. Excerpt from *Math Lesson Starters for the Common Core, Grades 6–8: Activities Aligned to the Standards and Assessments* by Paige Graiser, Ed.D.

Temperature Change

When Lauren woke up, the outside temperature was 72° Fahrenheit. At 1:00 p.m., the temperature had risen to 92°. To calculate the percent of change, Lauren set up the following proportion:

$$\frac{92 - 72 = 24}{100} = \frac{92}{x}$$

If Lauren solves her proportion for *x*, will she have determined the percent of change for the day's temperature?

If you think that Lauren's proportion is correct, use it to calculate the percent of change.

If you think that Lauren's proportion is incorrect, write the correct proportion and solve.

Copyright © 2014 Taylor & Francis. Excerpt from *Math Lesson Starters for the Common Core, Grades 6–8: Activities Aligned to the Standards and Assessments* by Paige Graiser, Ed.D.

Function Fun

....

Determine whether each relation is a function.

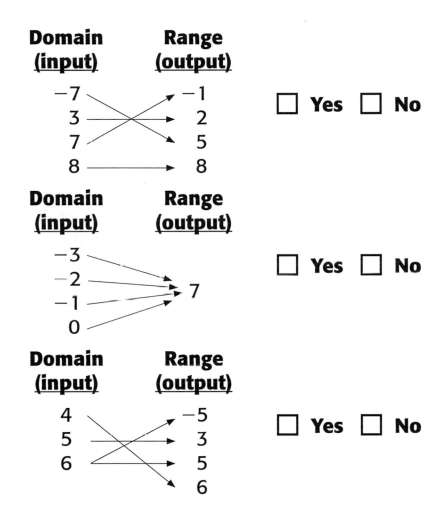

Domain (input)   **Range (output)**

−7   −1
3   2
7   5
8   8

☐ Yes   ☐ No

Domain (input)   **Range (output)**

−3
−2   7
−1
0

☐ Yes   ☐ No

Domain (input)   **Range (output)**

4   −5
5   3
6   5
   6

☐ Yes   ☐ No

Draw a model for the relation below and tell whether the relation is a function.

$\{(0, 5), (−2, 6), (0, −1), (5, 5)\}$ ☐ Yes   ☐ No

Copyright © 2014 Taylor & Francis. Excerpt from *Math Lesson Starters for the Common Core, Grades 6–8: Activities Aligned to the Standards and Assessments* by Paige Graiser, Ed.D.

A Taxing Phone Problem

Tabatha wants to buy a new smartphone. The phone will cost $121.00, and she will have to pay a $30.00 connection fee. Additionally, she will pay a 6½ percent tax on the cost of the phone.

Tabatha's Calculations	
Phone	121.00
Connection fee	30.00
Tax (6½%)	9.82
Total	$160.82

Do you agree with Tabatha's calculations? Has she correctly figured the amount she will have to pay to receive her new phone? What misconception does Tabatha have? Calculate the correct amount that Tabatha will have to pay for her new phone and phone service.

Copyright © 2014 Taylor & Francis. Excerpt from *Math Lesson Starters for the Common Core, Grades 6–8: Activities Aligned to the Standards and Assessments* by Paige Graiser, Ed.D.

Number Line Story Time

Examine each double number line below. Create a story that corresponds to each number line, and fill in the missing double number line values.

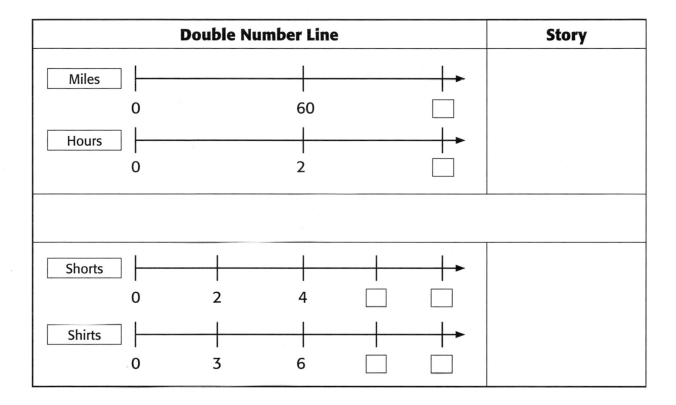

Double Number Line	Story
Miles: 0, 60, ☐ / Hours: 0, 2, ☐	
Shorts: 0, 2, 4, ☐, ☐ / Shirts: 0, 3, 6, ☐, ☐	

Copyright © 2014 Taylor & Francis. Excerpt from *Math Lesson Starters for the Common Core, Grades 6–8: Activities Aligned to the Standards and Assessments* by Paige Graiser, Ed.D.

Rearranging Interest

Hector knows that the formula for calculating simple interest is $I = prt$:

$$I = prt$$

I = interest

p = principal (the amount of money borrowed or invested)

r = rate (the rate of interest that is charged or earned)

t = time (the time in years that money is borrowed or invested)

Hector wants to know the formulas for finding the principal, the rate, or the time. Complete the table below:

What is the formula for calculating the principal? (solve for *p*)	What is the formula for calculating the rate? (solve for *r*)	What is the formula for calculating the time? (solve for *t*)

Copyright © 2014 Taylor & Francis. Excerpt from *Math Lesson Starters for the Common Core, Grades 6–8: Activities Aligned to the Standards and Assessments* by Paige Graiser, Ed.D.

Model House

Connor is building a scale model of his house. He is using a scale of 3 in : 2 ft.

If the actual height of Connor's house is 36 feet tall, how tall should he make his model? Explain how you calculated your answer.

Copyright © 2014 Taylor & Francis. Excerpt from *Math Lesson Starters for the Common Core, Grades 6–8: Activities Aligned to the Standards and Assessments* by Paige Graiser, Ed.D.

Unit Reflection

Ratios & Proportional Relationships

What worked well:

_____

_____

_____

_____

What I would do differently:

_____

_____

_____

_____

My next steps:

_____

_____

_____

_____

UNIT 2
CCSS-M Domain NS
The Number System

Mathematics is the queen of the sciences and number theory is the queen of mathematics.

Carl Friedrich Gauss

The Number System

Under the CCSS, students in the middle grades will begin working with the full system of rational numbers, including negative rational numbers, and negative integers. Most of the work in this domain will center around problem solving with all numbers in everyday situations. It is important that students begin to view negative numbers in everyday context such as temperature, distance below sea level, and money owed.

Students in middle-grades math will deepen their understanding of fractions, decimals, and percents and increase their mathematical fluency with these values. In addition to working with negative numbers, students' work within the coordinate plane is expanded to include all four quadrants.

Sixth Grade

In grade 6, students will begin to build on their understanding of place value and basic properties of operations to further explore fractions and negative numbers. Students will use their understanding of the relationship between multiplication and division to understand the division of fractions. Students in grade 6 will also begin working with the full system of rational numbers and begin exploring the concept of the distance from zero being a measurement of size (absolute value).

Seventh Grade

By grade 7, students will extend all four mathematical operations to all rational numbers. They will model, explain, and interpret the rules for adding, subtracting, multiplying, and dividing with negative numbers. They will use the basic arithmetic of rational numbers to begin to formulate simple expressions and equations in one variable. Students will use these equations to solve real-world problems that include rational numbers.

Eighth Grade

By the end of grade 8, students will understand that numbers that are not rational are considered to be irrational. They will also have an informal understanding that every number has a decimal expansion. Students will be able to convert a decimal expansion that repeats into a rational number. In grade 7, students encounter repeating decimals, but students in grade 8 will be able to explain why this occurs.

Key Vocabulary Terms: The Number System

Sixth Grade	Seventh Grade	Eighth Grade
greatest common factor	terminate	irrational number
least common multiple	additive inverse	decimal expansion
integer	multiplicative inverse	
positive number	equation	
negative number	expression	
opposite	term	
zero pair	variable	
absolute value	terminating decimal	
rational number	repeating decimal	

Vocabulary Notes

_____

_____

_____

_____

_____

_____

_____

_____

_____

Anticipating Adding and Subtracting Integers

Directions: Read each statement in the middle of the chart. On the left-hand side, labeled "Warm-Up," check if you agree or disagree with the statement. Leave the right-hand side, labeled "After Class," blank until your teacher instructs you to complete the assignment.

Warm-Up			After Class	
Agree	Disagree	Statement	Agree	Disagree
		The opposite of 10 is −10.		
		The absolute value of a number measures how far the number is from zero.		
		To subtract 12 − (−8) you "add the opposite," so the difference is 20.		
		When adding a positive and a negative integer, always take the sign of the larger integer.		
		The difference of two positive numbers is always positive.		

Copyright © 2014 Taylor & Francis. Excerpt from *Math Lesson Starters for the Common Core, Grades 6–8: Activities Aligned to the Standards and Assessments* by Paige Graiser, Ed.D.

Rational and Irrational Number Sort

In his math class, Gordon learned about rational and irrational numbers. For homework, he was asked to sort the following values into a table.

Gordon's Homework	
Rational Numbers	Irrational Numbers
3.0 −7 $8\frac{2}{3}$	√9 √2 π

Do you <u>agree</u> with Gordon? If not, what changes would you make? What does Gordon not understand about rational and irrational numbers?

Copyright © 2014 Taylor & Francis. Excerpt from *Math Lesson Starters for the Common Core, Grades 6–8: Activities Aligned to the Standards and Assessments* by Paige Graiser, Ed.D.

Fractions and Decimals

Fill in the missing values in the chart below:

Fraction	Decimal Expansion	Does the Decimal Repeat or Terminate?
	$0.\overline{3}$	**Repeats**
$\dfrac{1}{20}$		
$\dfrac{1}{11}$		
	0.2	**Terminates**
$\dfrac{1}{9}$		
	0.1	**Terminates**

Math Fact

*The line drawn above a set of repeating decimals (such as $0.\overline{125}$) is called a **vinculum**.*

Copyright © 2014 Taylor & Francis. Excerpt from *Math Lesson Starters for the Common Core, Grades 6–8: Activities Aligned to the Standards and Assessments* by Paige Graiser, Ed.D.

Jumpstart: Integers

Complete the table by performing each operation indicated across the top with each pair of numbers in the column on the left. Make sure you use the pairs of numbers in the order that they are given. The first row has been done for you.

	Add	Subtract	Multiply	Divide
3, 2	$3 + 2$ **5**	$3 - 2$ **3**	$3 \cdot 2$ **6**	$3 \div 2$ **3/2**
4, 4				
−4, (−4)				
−4, 4				
4, −4				

Math Trivia

40 (forty) is the only number whose letters are in alphabetical order.

Copyright © 2014 Taylor & Francis. Excerpt from *Math Lesson Starters for the Common Core, Grades 6–8: Activities Aligned to the Standards and Assessments* by Paige Graiser, Ed.D.

Anticipating Division of Rational Numbers

Directions: Read each statement in the middle of the chart. On the left-hand side, labeled "Warm-Up," check if you agree or disagree with the statement. Leave the right-hand side, labeled "After Class," blank until your teacher instructs you to complete the assignment.

| Warm-Up | | | After Class | |
Agree	Disagree	Statement	Agree	Disagree
		3/4 is the reciprocal of 4/3.		
		2/1 is the reciprocal of 1/2.		
		1/2 is the reciprocal of 2.		
		Dividing by 1/2 produces the same result as multiplying by 2.		
		Dividing by 3/4 produces the same result as multiplying by 4/3.		
		When you multiply fractions, you must have the same denominator first.		

Copyright © 2014 Taylor & Francis. Excerpt from *Math Lesson Starters for the Common Core, Grades 6–8: Activities Aligned to the Standards and Assessments* by Paige Graiser, Ed.D.

Ordering Rational Numbers

Lorenzo completed each problem below by placing a $=$, $<$ or $>$ in the box to make each sentence true.

Check Lorenzo's work. For each problem, determine if he is correct or incorrect.

a.	$5/6$ $\boxed{=}$ $10/12$	☐ Correct	☐ Incorrect
b.	-7 $\boxed{>}$ -5	☐ Correct	☐ Incorrect
c.	$2/5$ $\boxed{>}$ $2/3$	☐ Correct	☐ Incorrect
d.	$-4\frac{1}{2}$ $\boxed{<}$ $-7/2$	☐ Correct	☐ Incorrect
e.	0 $\boxed{<}$ -9	☐ Correct	☐ Incorrect

For each incorrect problem, explain what was wrong with Lorenzo's thinking.

Copyright © 2014 Taylor & Francis. Excerpt from *Math Lesson Starters for the Common Core, Grades 6–8: Activities Aligned to the Standards and Assessments* by Paige Graiser, Ed.D.

Fractions, Decimals, and Percents

Fill in the missing values.

	Fraction	Decimal	Percent
a.			74.3%
b.		0.373	
c.	15/16		
d.		.0029	

Copyright © 2014 Taylor & Francis. Excerpt from *Math Lesson Starters for the Common Core, Grades 6–8: Activities Aligned to the Standards and Assessments* by Paige Graiser, Ed.D.

Write about It: Reasonable Answers

What does *reasonable* mean? When solving a word problem, why is it important to check your answers for reasonableness? Create a word problem, and give an example of an unreasonable answer that a student might come up with, as well as the correct answer to your problem.

Copyright © 2014 Taylor & Francis. Excerpt from *Math Lesson Starters for the Common Core, Grades 6–8: Activities Aligned to the Standards and Assessments* by Paige Graiser, Ed.D.

Sometimes, Always, or Never: Adding and Multiplying

Determine if the following statement is sometimes true, always true, or never true. Please show proof of your choice.

When you add two numbers, you get the same answer that you get when you multiply the two numbers. $x + y = xy$	☐ Sometimes True ☐ Always True ☐ Never True	My proof:

Copyright © 2014 Taylor & Francis. Excerpt from *Math Lesson Starters for the Common Core, Grades 6–8: Activities Aligned to the Standards and Assessments* by Paige Graiser, Ed.D.

Graphing Irrational Numbers

Think about the value of √3. Graph the √3 on the following number line.

Think about the value of √6. Graph the √6 on the following number line.

Math Fact
There is no Roman numeral for zero.

Copyright © 2014 Taylor & Francis. Excerpt from *Math Lesson Starters for the Common Core, Grades 6–8: Activities Aligned to the Standards and Assessments* by Paige Graiser, Ed.D.

A Negative Discussion

Alex and Elizabeth were discussing the following values:

$$-\frac{1}{4} \qquad \frac{-1}{4} \qquad \frac{1}{-4}$$

Alex says:
These numbers do not mean the same thing.

Elizabeth says:
These numbers are all equal.

Who is correct?

If you believe that Alex is correct, draw a number line and graph each quantity.

If you believe that Elizabeth is correct, explain in your own words how the three quantities can represent the same quantity.

Math Trivia

Many buildings in China do not have a 4th floor. The Chinese word for 4 sounds like the Chinese word for death.

Copyright © 2014 Taylor & Francis. Excerpt from *Math Lesson Starters for the Common Core, Grades 6–8: Activities Aligned to the Standards and Assessments* by Paige Graiser, Ed.D.

Absolute Value Homework

Hank completed the following absolute value problems for homework. Check over his answers, and determine if they are correct. If Hank is wrong, correct his answers.

	Correct	Incorrect	Correct Answer
$|8| = 8$			
$|-8| = -8$			
$|-3| < |-6|$			
$|4 + 2(-4)| = 24$			
$|-xy^2| = -xy^2$			

Math Fact

Absolute value symbols are actually called *bars*.

Copyright © 2014 Taylor & Francis. Excerpt from *Math Lesson Starters for the Common Core, Grades 6–8: Activities Aligned to the Standards and Assessments* by Paige Graiser, Ed.D.

Mental Math: Number Sense

Calculate the following using only your mind—*no calculators, no paper, no pencils.*

- Start with the number of months in a year.
- Multiply that number by 10.
- Divide that number by the absolute value of −30.
- Square that number.
- Divide that number by the opposite of 4.
- Divide the result by −1.
- What is your answer?

Math Fact

The symbol for division (÷) is called an obelus.

Copyright © 2014 Taylor & Francis. Excerpt from *Math Lesson Starters for the Common Core, Grades 6–8: Activities Aligned to the Standards and Assessments* by Paige Graiser, Ed.D.

Decimal Expansion: What's Missing?

Jace was asked to write 248.6529 on the board in expanded form. He is missing a few numbers. Help Jace complete the problem.

$$248.6529 = (2 \times 100) + (4 \times \boxed{}) + (\boxed{} \times 1) +$$

$$(6 \times \frac{1}{10}) + (5 \times \boxed{}) + (\boxed{} \times \frac{1}{1000}) + (9 \times \boxed{})$$

Math Trivia

The term Googol (10^{100}, or 10 followed by 100 zeroes) was coined in 1938 by a nine-year-old boy named Milton Sirotta.

Copyright © 2014 Taylor & Francis. Excerpt from *Math Lesson Starters for the Common Core, Grades 6–8: Activities Aligned to the Standards and Assessments* by Paige Graiser, Ed.D.

LCM and GCF Fill-In

Fill in the missing words from the sentences below. Use the words provided.

The _____ is the smallest number that two or more numbers will divide into _____.

The _____ number that divides exactly into two or more numbers is called the _____.

_____ numbers can be written as the product of _____ numbers.

This is called prime _____.

factorization   composite   zero   least common multiple

evenly   greatest common factor   prime   largest

Copyright © 2014 Taylor & Francis. Excerpt from *Math Lesson Starters for the Common Core, Grades 6–8: Activities Aligned to the Standards and Assessments* by Paige Graiser, Ed.D.

Finding Factors of Monomials

Xavier was calculating the greatest common factor for $24x^2y$ and $36xy^2$. He wrote each monomial as a product of prime factors. His work is below:

$$24x^2y = 2 \cdot 2 \cdot 2 \cdot 3 \cdot x \cdot x \cdot y$$

$$36xy^2 = 2 \cdot 2 \cdot 3 \cdot 3 \cdot x \cdot y \cdot y$$

a. Check Xavier's work to see if he has correctly written the monomials as a product of prime factors.

b. Xavier has forgotten the next step in factoring monomials. Explain in your own words how to complete the factorization.

Copyright © 2014 Taylor & Francis. Excerpt from *Math Lesson Starters for the Common Core, Grades 6–8: Activities Aligned to the Standards and Assessments* by Paige Graiser, Ed.D.

Write a Like Term

For each term below, write a like term. The first one has been done for you.

Term	Like Term
$-4x$	$6x$
$-2xy$	
$3x^2$	
7	
xy^2	
$\frac{1}{4}x^2y^2$	

Math Trivia

In the numbers 0 through 1,000, the letter A appears only
once (one-thousand)

Copyright © 2014 Taylor & Francis. Excerpt from *Math Lesson Starters for the Common Core, Grades 6–8: Activities Aligned to the Standards and Assessments* by Paige Graiser, Ed.D.

Unit Reflection
The Number System

What worked well:

_____

_____

_____

_____

_____

What I would do differently:

_____

_____

_____

_____

_____

My next steps:

_____

_____

_____

_____

_____

UNIT 3
CCSS-M Domain EE
Expressions & Equations

*The human mind has never invented
a labor-saving machine equal to algebra.*

Author Unknown

Expressions & Equations

During the middle grades, students will develop an understanding of the use of variables in mathematical expressions and equations. The introduction of variables into mathematics tends to be a sticking point for many students (and their parents), but this will not be a new concept since all elementary students are asked to solve problems such as $2 + \square = 7$ or $8 - ? = 5$ (with $\square$ and ? acting as variables in these examples).

Student work in this standard will include writing expressions that correspond to given situations, the evaluation of expressions, and the use of formulas to solve real-world problems. Students will learn that the solutions of an equation are the number values of the variables that make the equation true. Students will also use the notion of maintaining the balance of both sides of an equation to solve equations. Students in grade 6 will begin solving one-step equations but will progress to multistep equations by grade 7.

Sixth Grade

In grade 6, students will begin to understand the use of variables in mathematical expressions. They will write simple expressions and equations that correspond to real-world situations, evaluate expressions, and use expressions and simple formulas to solve real-world problems. Students will learn that the solutions of an equation are the values that can be assigned to the variables that make an equation true. To round out their study of expressions and equations, sixth-grade students will construct and analyze tables and will use equations (such as $6x = y$) to describe the relationships between quantities.

Seventh Grade

Students in grade 7 will progress to solving multistep real-life problems that involve both positive and negative rational numbers. These problems will contain whole numbers, fractions, and decimals. By grade 7, students must be able to calculate with numbers in any form and convert between number forms when needed (e.g., fraction to percent, percent to decimal). Students will also be required to appraise the reasonableness of their answers using mental computation and estimation.

Eighth Grade

Students in grade 8 will use linear equations and systems of linear equations to solve a variety of problems. Students will recognize special linear equations (such as $y = mx + b$) and understand that the slope (m) of a line is a constant rate of change. Students will also use linear equations to describe the association between two quantities (such as foot length vs. height for a classroom of students). Students will also use linear equations, systems of linear equations, and linear functions as well as their understanding of slope to analyze situations and solve real-world problems. At grade 8, students also explore operations with numbers in scientific notation.

Key Vocabulary Terms: Expressions & Equations

Sixth Grade	Seventh Grade	Eighth Grade
variable	inequality	integer exponent
term	estimation	square root
algebraic expression		cube root
equation		scientific notation
formula		slope
order of operations		linear equation
dependent variable		slope-intercept form
independent variable		
reciprocal		

Vocabulary Notes

Equation Selection

William's teacher asked the class to write the following as an algebraic equation:

10 less than a number is 5

William wrote two possible answers on his paper:

$$10 - x = 5$$

$$x - 10 = 5$$

What is one question you could ask William that would help to clarify his thinking and assist him in selecting the correct answer?

Copyright © 2014 Taylor & Francis. Excerpt from *Math Lesson Starters for the Common Core, Grades 6–8: Activities Aligned to the Standards and Assessments* by Paige Graiser, Ed.D.

Jumpstart: Variables

Complete the table by performing each operation indicated across the top with each pair of numbers and/or variables in the column on the left. Make sure you use each pair of numbers or variables in the order that they are given. Simplify your signs when possible. The first row has been done for you.

	Add	Subtract	Multiply	Divide
x, y	$x + y$	$x - y$	xy	x/y
$-x, -y$				
$x, -y$				
x, x				

Copyright © 2014 Taylor & Francis. Excerpt from *Math Lesson Starters for the Common Core, Grades 6–8: Activities Aligned to the Standards and Assessments* by Paige Graiser, Ed.D.

Expression Match-Up

Match each expression with its written statement:

$2x + 4$	**Four less than twice x**
$2x - 4$	**Four more than twice x**
$2(x + 2)$	**Twice the sum of x and four**
$2(x + 4)$	**Twice the difference of x and four**
$2(x - 4)$	

Teaching Tip

Consider copying this activity onto cardstock and having the students cut out and match the expressions with the written statements.

Copyright © 2014 Taylor & Francis. Excerpt from *Math Lesson Starters for the Common Core, Grades 6–8: Activities Aligned to the Standards and Assessments* by Paige Graiser, Ed.D.

What's the Difference?

Each of the values below contains an 8 and four zeroes:

80,000		8.0000

a. Explain in your own words what each of the above values represents.
b. Which of the following symbols would you put in the center box to make a true statement?

$$(<, \leq, >, \text{ or } \geq)$$

c. Write each of the above values in scientific notation.

Copyright © 2014 Taylor & Francis. Excerpt from *Math Lesson Starters for the Common Core, Grades 6–8: Activities Aligned to the Standards and Assessments* by Paige Graiser, Ed.D.

Equation Fill-In

Fill in the missing words from the sentences below. Use the words provided.

An _____ is a mathematical phrase that combines _____ and/or variables using mathematical _____.

An _____ is a mathematical statement that two things are equal. It consists of two _____, one on each side of an equals sign.

A _____ is a special type of equation that shows the relationship between different _____.

variables   expressions   operations   expression

formula   equation   numbers

Copyright © 2014 Taylor & Francis. Excerpt from *Math Lesson Starters for the Common Core, Grades 6–8: Activities Aligned to the Standards and Assessments* by Paige Graiser, Ed.D.

Write about It: Calculating Steps

How could you calculate the number of minutes you have spent in school? What information would you need to consider? Describe the steps you would follow to calculate the time you have spent in school (you do not have to actually calculate the answer).

Copyright © 2014 Taylor & Francis. Excerpt from *Math Lesson Starters for the Common Core, Grades 6–8: Activities Aligned to the Standards and Assessments* by Paige Graiser, Ed.D.

What Am I?

With a check mark in the appropriate column, classify each of the following as an expression, equation, or formula:

	Expression	Equation	Formula
$5 + x = 12$			
$V = (l) (w) (h)$			
$w = V / (h) (l)$			
$16y = 48$			
$a + b - c$			
$a^2 + b^2 = c^2$			
$8 + 3^4$			
$n/9 = 15$			

Hint

A formula is a special type of equation. Formulas show a relationship between two or more variables.

Copyright © 2014 Taylor & Francis. Excerpt from *Math Lesson Starters for the Common Core, Grades 6–8: Activities Aligned to the Standards and Assessments* by Paige Graiser, Ed.D.

The Power of Parentheses

Zola is having a difficult time understanding how parentheses affect mathematical expressions. She considers the following expressions and decides that they are equal:

a. Select a value for the variable n, and evaluate each expression. What did you get for each?
b. Do you agree with Zola?
c. How would you explain the differences between the two expressions to Zola?

Math Fact

The equals sign (=) was invented by mathematician Robert Recorde in 1557.

Copyright © 2014 Taylor & Francis. Excerpt from *Math Lesson Starters for the Common Core, Grades 6–8: Activities Aligned to the Standards and Assessments* by Paige Graiser, Ed.D.

Mental Math: Linear Equations

Calculate the following using only your mind—*no calculators, no paper, no pencils.*

- Consider the equation $y = 4x + 8$.
- Start with the *y*-intercept.
- Subtract the slope of the line.
- Add the value of *y* when $x = \frac{1}{2}$.
- Add the value of *x* when $y = -4$.
- What is your answer?

Copyright © 2014 Taylor & Francis. Excerpt from *Math Lesson Starters for the Common Core, Grades 6–8: Activities Aligned to the Standards and Assessments* by Paige Graiser, Ed.D.

Reciprocal Riddle

What happens when you take the *reciprocal* of a *reciprocal*? Explain in your own words.

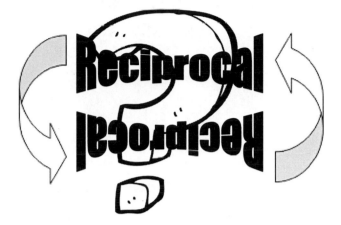

Hint
A number times its reciprocal (or multiplicative inverse) is equal to 1. For example, the reciprocal of $\frac{2}{3}$ is $\frac{3}{2}$.

Copyright © 2014 Taylor & Francis. Excerpt from *Math Lesson Starters for the Common Core, Grades 6–8: Activities Aligned to the Standards and Assessments* by Paige Graiser, Ed.D.

Inequality Flip?

For each inequality in the table below, check whether you need to reverse the inequality symbol.

	YES	NO
$3x < -12$		
$-2c > -10$		
$-5m \geq -20$		
$\dfrac{a}{-7} < 2$		

Hint

Whenever you multiply or divide by a negative number, you have to reverse the inequality symbol.

Copyright © 2014 Taylor & Francis. Excerpt from *Math Lesson Starters for the Common Core, Grades 6–8: Activities Aligned to the Standards and Assessments* by Paige Graiser, Ed.D.

Scientific Notation Reports

Spencer is writing a report for his science class on the sun. He found from his research that the mass of the sun is 2,000,000,000,000,000,000,000,000,000,000 kg. When typing his report, he decides to use scientific notation to represent this number:

$$20 \times 10^{29}$$

Madison is writing a report on the human body. She found out that red blood cells have a diameter of .00075 centimeters. This is how she wrote this number in scientific notation:

$$7.5 \times 10^{4}$$

Do you agree with Spencer's and Madison's thinking? Why or why not?

a. What errors have they made?

b. Using scientific notation, write the correct form of each number.

Math Fact

After trillion comes quadrillion, quintillion, sextillion, septillion, octillion, and nonillion.

Copyright © 2014 Taylor & Francis. Excerpt from *Math Lesson Starters for the Common Core, Grades 6–8: Activities Aligned to the Standards and Assessments* by Paige Graiser, Ed.D.

Order Matters

Mrs. Klein wrote the following problems on the board:

$$4 + 7 \times 3 =$$
$$(4 + 7) \times 3 =$$
$$4 + (7 \times 3) =$$

Chris says:

All of the problems have the same answer because it does not matter which order you add or multiply numbers because addition and multiplication are commutative.

a. What are the answers to the problems? Do they all have the same answer?

b. What is wrong with Chris's thinking? How would you explain the correct answers to Chris?

Copyright © 2014 Taylor & Francis. Excerpt from *Math Lesson Starters for the Common Core, Grades 6–8: Activities Aligned to the Standards and Assessments* by Paige Graiser, Ed.D.

Anticipating Linear Equations in Two Variables

Directions: Read each statement in the middle of the chart. On the left-hand side, labeled "Warm-Up," check if you agree or disagree with the statement. Leave the right-hand side, labeled "After Class," blank until your teacher instructs you to complete the assignment.

Warm-Up			After Class	
Agree	Disagree	Statement	Agree	Disagree
		The graph of a linear equation is a line.		
		The solution set for any linear equation in x and y is exactly one ordered pair.		
		The slope of a vertical line is zero.		
		Slope-intercept form looks like: $y = mx + b$.		
		Two parallel lines have equal slopes.		

Copyright © 2014 Taylor & Francis. Excerpt from *Math Lesson Starters for the Common Core, Grades 6–8: Activities Aligned to the Standards and Assessments* by Paige Graiser, Ed.D.

Applying Slope

The figure shown is a square.

The equation of line *wz* is $y = -\dfrac{1}{3}x + 2$.

$$y = -\frac{1}{3}x + 2.$$

Using what you know about line *mp*, find the following:

a. The slope of line *xy* _____

b. The slope of line *wx* _____

c. The slope of line *zy* _____

Math Fact

When constructing a roof, builders calculate *pitch* rather than slope (a mathematical term).

Slope, pitch, and steepness all mean the same thing.

Copyright © 2014 Taylor & Francis. Excerpt from *Math Lesson Starters for the Common Core, Grades 6–8: Activities Aligned to the Standards and Assessments* by Paige Graiser, Ed.D.

Unit Reflection
Expressions & Equations

What worked well:

_____

_____

_____

_____

_____

What I would do differently:

_____

_____

_____

_____

_____

My next steps:

_____

_____

_____

_____

_____

UNIT 4
CCSS-M Domain G
Geometry

The description of right lines and circles, upon which geometry is founded, belongs to mechanics. Geometry does not teach us to draw these lines, but requires them to be drawn.

Sir Isaac Newton

Geometry

Geometry is the only CCSS-M domain that remains constant from kindergarten through high school. Other domains morph into new domains as students move from elementary school to middle school. For example, the K–5 Measurement and Data Domain becomes Statistics and Probability for grades 6–12. Geometry is the only constant progression in the CCSS-M.

The focus of the geometry domain moves from identification of basic shapes to constructions, identification of relationships between shapes, work with scale drawings, and the use of more complex formulas for area and volume. Teachers can expect their students to face geometric problems rooted in real-world and career connections (such as carpentry, architecture, and medicine) on CCSS-M–based assessments.

Sixth Grade

Students entering grade 6 will build on their elementary understanding of length, area, and volume. Additionally, students in sixth grade will compute the area of right triangles and other special figures and calculate the volume of right rectangular prisms. In many instances, students will be working with dimensions that are not given in whole numbers. Students will prepare for work on scale drawings and constructions by drawing polygons in the coordinate plane when given coordinates for the vertices. Students will also represent three-dimensional figures using nets constructed of rectangles and triangles. The nets will be used to find the surface area of these figures.

Seventh Grade

In grade 7, students will apply their understanding of length and area in applying formulas for the circumference and area of circles and the volume and surface area of three-dimensional figures. They will solve mathematical problems involving area, surface area, and volume of two- and three-dimensional objects composed of triangles, quadrilaterals, polygons, cubes, and right prisms. Additionally, students will begin to explore the relationships between angles formed by intersecting lines.

Eighth Grade

By grade 8, students will apply their understanding of volume to learning and using formulas to find the volumes of cones, cylinders, and spheres. Students will understand the Pythagorean Theorem and its converse and will model the Pythagorean Theorem by decomposing a square in two different ways. They will apply the Pythagorean Theorem to find distances between points on the coordinate plane, to find lengths, and to analyze other polygons. To round out their study of geometry, students in grade 8 will apply their knowledge of distance and angles to model how they behave under translations, rotations, reflections, and dilations. They will also use congruence and similarity to describe and analyze two-dimensional figures.

Key Vocabulary Terms: Geometry

Sixth Grade	Seventh Grade	Eighth Grade
base	scale drawing	congruent
nets	plane sections	translation
acute triangle	circumference	similar figures
equilateral triangle	supplementary angles	transversal
obtuse triangle	complementary angles	corresponding angles
prism	vertical angles	interior
pyramid	adjacent angles	exterior
right triangle		Pythagorean Theorem
scalene triangle		
surface area		
volume		

Vocabulary Notes

Describe the Difference

Describe the difference between a square and a rectangle.	
Describe the difference between a diamond and a square.	
Describe the difference between a circle and an oval.	

Underline all of the math terms you used in your descriptions.

Copyright © 2014 Taylor & Francis. Excerpt from *Math Lesson Starters for the Common Core, Grades 6–8: Activities Aligned to the Standards and Assessments* by Paige Graiser, Ed.D.

Analogies: Geometry Terms

An analogy is a word problem that is made up of two word pairs. Here is an example:

Summer is to *hot* as *winter* is to _____.

To complete the analogy, you must find a word that has the same relationship to "winter" as "hot" has to "summer." <u>Cold</u> is the best word to complete the analogy.

Using the word list on the left, choose the best word to complete each analogy on the right.

a. A circle is to a square as circumference is to _____.

b. A _____ is to a circle as a protractor is to an angle.

c. A reflection is to a flip as a _____ is to a turn.

d. A ray is to a _____ as an arc is to a circle.

e. A square is to a cube as a circle is to a _____.

line

rotation

parallel

compass

point

cylinder

perimeter

Copyright © 2014 Taylor & Francis. Excerpt from *Math Lesson Starters for the Common Core, Grades 6–8: Activities Aligned to the Standards and Assessments* by Paige Graiser, Ed.D.

Do You Know Your Geometry Symbols?

Translate the meaning of each geometry symbol into words. The first one has been done for you.

● p $point\ p$	$\overline{ab}$	$\overleftrightarrow{ab}$	$\overrightarrow{ab}$
$m\angle A$	ab ∥ cd	ab ⊥ cd	Using symbols, write the following: Angle A is congruent to Angle B.

Copyright © 2014 Taylor & Francis. Excerpt from *Math Lesson Starters for the Common Core, Grades 6–8: Activities Aligned to the Standards and Assessments* by Paige Graiser, Ed.D.

Sometimes, Always, or Never: Polygons

Determine if the following statement is sometimes true, always true, or never true. Please show proof of your choice.

In a regular polygon, the number of sides is equal to the number of lines of symmetry.	☐ Sometimes True ☐ Always True ☐ Never True	My proof:

Equilateral Triangle

Square

Regular Pentagon

Regular Hexagon

Regular Heptagon

Regular Octagon

Regular Nonagon

Regular Decagon

Copyright © 2014 Taylor & Francis. Excerpt from *Math Lesson Starters for the Common Core, Grades 6–8: Activities Aligned to the Standards and Assessments* by Paige Graiser, Ed.D.

Pythagoras's Candy Shop

Pythagoras was giving out samples of his delicious candy bars. Each customer could choose either

<u>One large</u> candy bar (*c*)

      or

<u>Both small</u> candy bars (*a* and *b*).

Would you choose the large candy bar? Or would you choose to take the two smaller bars? Explain your choice.

$$a^2+b^2=c^2$$

Math Trivia

Pythagoras was a Greek philosopher who lived around 500 B.C.

Copyright © 2014 Taylor & Francis. Excerpt from *Math Lesson Starters for the Common Core, Grades 6–8: Activities Aligned to the Standards and Assessments* by Paige Graiser, Ed.D.

Triangle Sketching I: Sides

Below you will find descriptions of triangles. Sketch each triangle, and label it with the correct term from the list provided.

Description	Your Sketch	Label
A. Draw a triangle with all sides having the same length.		
B. Draw a triangle that has two sides that are the same length.		
C. Draw a triangle that has no sides that are the same length.		

Label Choices:

Isosceles	**Equilateral**	**Scalene**

Teaching Tip

Have pairs of students compare their drawings and labels.

CCSS-M Domain G: Geometry   **81**

Copyright © 2014 Taylor & Francis. Excerpt from *Math Lesson Starters for the Common Core, Grades 6–8: Activities Aligned to the Standards and Assessments* by Paige Graiser, Ed.D.

Triangle Sketching II: Angles

Below you will find descriptions of triangles. Sketch each triangle, and label it with the correct term from the list provided.

Description	Your Sketch	Label
A. Draw a triangle in which all of the angles are less than 90 degrees.		
B. Draw a triangle that has one 90-degree angle.		
C. Draw a triangle that has one angle that is greater than 90 degrees.		

Label Choices:

Right   **Obtuse**   **Acute**

Teaching Tip

Have pairs of students compare their drawings and labels.

Copyright © 2014 Taylor & Francis. Excerpt from *Math Lesson Starters for the Common Core, Grades 6–8: Activities Aligned to the Standards and Assessments* by Paige Graiser, Ed.D.

Feature Analysis: Polygons

Consider each of the figures below. For each figure, read each feature and determine if the figure has that feature. If so, place an X in the box. The first one has been done for you.

Feature

		Equilateral	Equiangular	4-sided	3-sided	Opposite Sides Parallel
Square		X	X	X		X
Rectangle						
Triangle						
Quadrilateral						
Rhombus						
Trapezoid						

Copyright © 2014 Taylor & Francis. Excerpt from *Math Lesson Starters for the Common Core, Grades 6–8: Activities Aligned to the Standards and Assessments* by Paige Graiser, Ed.D.

Shape-Shifting Matrix

Complete the table below.

Polygon	Number of Sides	Number of Angles	Sum of All Interior Angles	Sum of Each Angle
Equilateral Triangle	3	3	180°	60°
Square				
Regular Pentagon				
Regular Hexagon				
Regular Octagon				
Regular Polygon with n Sides	n			

Copyright © 2014 Taylor & Francis. Excerpt from *Math Lesson Starters for the Common Core, Grades 6–8: Activities Aligned to the Standards and Assessments* by Paige Graiser, Ed.D.

Mental Math: Geometry

Calculate the following using only your mind—*no calculators, no paper, no pencils.*

- Start with the number of sides in a pentagon.
- Multiply by the number of diagonals in a square.
- Divide by the square root of the number of sides in a quadrilateral.
- Add the number of sides in an octagon.
- Double your number.
- What is your answer?

Copyright © 2014 Taylor & Francis. Excerpt from *Math Lesson Starters for the Common Core, Grades 6–8: Activities Aligned to the Standards and Assessments* by Paige Graiser, Ed.D.

Circle Fill-In

Fill in the missing words from the sentences below. Use the words provided.

A circle is named by its center _____.

The distance across a circle through its _____ is called the _____.

The _____ of a circle is the distance from the center point to any point on the circle.

The distance around a circle is called the _____.

The length of two _____ is equal to one _____.

radius	circumference	point	center

diameter	radii

Math Fact

Of all shapes with the same area, the circle has the shortest perimeter.

Copyright © 2014 Taylor & Francis. Excerpt from *Math Lesson Starters for the Common Core, Grades 6–8: Activities Aligned to the Standards and Assessments* by Paige Graiser, Ed.D.

Angle-*ing*

Check whether each angle is acute, obtuse, or straight.

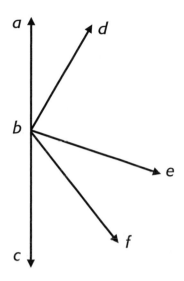

Angle	Acute	Obtuse	Straight
abd			
abe			
dbc			
abc			
dbf			
ebf			

Copyright © 2014 Taylor & Francis. Excerpt from *Math Lesson Starters for the Common Core, Grades 6–8: Activities Aligned to the Standards and Assessments* by Paige Graiser, Ed.D.

Line-Up

Use the drawing to the right to complete the table below by listing pairs of lines.

Line *b* is parallel to line *c*.

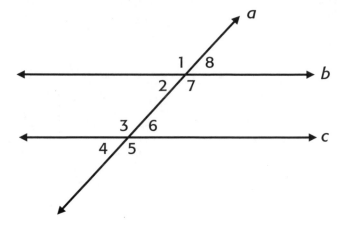

Complementary Angles	Supplementary Angles	Corresponding Angles	Alternate Interior Angles	Alternate Exterior Angles

Copyright © 2014 Taylor & Francis. Excerpt from *Math Lesson Starters for the Common Core, Grades 6–8: Activities Aligned to the Standards and Assessments* by Paige Graiser, Ed.D.

Write about It: Area and Perimeter

Explain the difference between the area of a backyard and the perimeter of a backyard. Why might a person need to know the area or perimeter of her backyard? Give examples of why someone would need to know these measurements.

Reasons for Knowing the Area of a Backyard	Reasons for Knowing the Perimeter of a Backyard

Copyright © 2014 Taylor & Francis. Excerpt from *Math Lesson Starters for the Common Core, Grades 6–8: Activities Aligned to the Standards and Assessments* by Paige Graiser, Ed.D.

Volume of Cubes

If the side length of this cube is doubled, what will happen to its volume?

a. The volume of the cube will double.

b. The volume of the cube will increase to four times its original volume.

c. The volume of the cube will increase to eight times its original volume

d. The volume of the cube will increase to 64 times its original volume

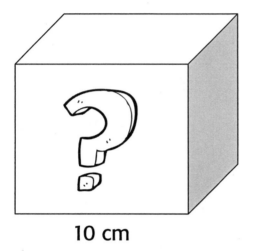

10 cm

Explain your reasoning.

Copyright © 2014 Taylor & Francis. Excerpt from *Math Lesson Starters for the Common Core, Grades 6–8: Activities Aligned to the Standards and Assessments* by Paige Graiser, Ed.D.

Rate Your Knowledge: Angle Relationships

Think about the terms listed in this chart. Put an X in the boxes that best describe your knowledge of each term.

	I Can Give a Definition	I Can Give an Example	I Can Draw a Picture	I Have No Idea
Transversal				
Complementary Angles				
Supplementary Angles				
Vertical Angles				
Interior Angles				
Corresponding Angles				

Teaching Tip

Knowledge-rating activities allow students to access and assess their prior knowledge. They are a great strategy to use at the beginning of a new unit of instruction.

Copyright © 2014 Taylor & Francis. Excerpt from *Math Lesson Starters for the Common Core, Grades 6–8: Activities Aligned to the Standards and Assessments* by Paige Graiser, Ed.D.

Anticipating Angles

Directions: Read each statement in the middle of the chart. On the left-hand side, labeled "Warm-Up," check if you agree or disagree with the statement. Leave the right-hand side, labeled "After Class," blank until your teacher instructs you to complete the assignment.

Warm-Up			After Class	
Agree	Disagree	Statement	Agree	Disagree
		An angle is made up of two sides and a vertex.		
		Angles are measured in units called degrees.		
		Acute angles have a measure greater than 90 degrees.		
		Obtuse angles have a measure that is less than 90 degrees.		
		Right angles measure exactly 90 degrees.		
		There is no such thing as a straight angle.		

Copyright © 2014 Taylor & Francis. Excerpt from *Math Lesson Starters for the Common Core, Grades 6–8: Activities Aligned to the Standards and Assessments* by Paige Graiser, Ed.D.

Unit Reflection
Geometry

What worked well:

_____

_____

_____

_____

_____

What I would do differently:

_____

_____

_____

_____

_____

My next steps:

_____

_____

_____

_____

_____

UNIT 5
CCSS-M Domain SP
Statistics & Probability

Be able to analyze statistics, which can be used to support or undercut almost any argument.

Marilyn vos Savant

Statistics & Probability

Statistical literacy is a critical skill in today's society and an important tool in allowing people to think and make good decisions for themselves. As students enter the middle grades, they progress from their elementary-level study of data collection through measurement to the more advanced topics of statistics and probability. Students will continue their study of this domain through grade 12.

As they enter the study of this CCSS-M domain at grade 6, students are focused on describing the distribution of sets of data. At grade 7, they progress to comparing sets of data and begin to look at sampling methods. By grade 8, students round out their middle-grades study of statistics and probability by analyzing bivariate data and constructing models.

Sixth Grade

Students in grade 6 will focus on developing their ability to think statistically. It is important that students not only calculate statistical measures but also develop statistical reasoning. Through their study of measures of central tendency, students will begin to summarize and describe single numerical sets of data by identifying clusters, peaks, gaps, and symmetry. Students will also focus on the context in which data is gathered. Again, the types of data that students collect and/or explore should relate to real-world experiences. Additionally, students show a higher level of engagement when working with data that they can relate to than when using sets of "canned" data often found in textbooks.

Seventh Grade

Building on their experiences from grade 6, students in grade 7 will explore multiple data distributions and explore differences in populations. They will begin to investigate the concept of random sampling to gather data and to draw inferences. Students in grade 7 will begin a more formal study of probability as they are introduced to the concept of chance and begin to develop and investigate probability models. Students will also explore the probabilities of compound events by using lists, tables, and simulations.

Eighth Grade

Students in grade 8 will explore data that involves two different variables whose values can change. Their analysis of these bivariate data will focus on describing patterns such as clustering, outliers, and positive or negative association, as well as linear association and nonlinear association. To assist with their analysis of these related sets of data, students will construct and interpret scatter plots and two-way tables for summarizing data on two variables collected from the same subject.

Key Vocabulary Terms: Statistics & Probability

Sixth Grade	Seventh Grade	Eighth Grade
mean	sample population	scatter plot
median	random sampling	outlier
mode	variability	positive association
range	probability	negative association
histogram	frequency	line of best fit
dot plot	sample event	
box plot	compound event	
mean absolute derivation	tree diagram	
interquartile range	simulation	
	permutations	
	combinations	

Vocabulary Notes

_____

_____

_____

_____

_____

_____

_____

Rate Your Knowledge: Statistics

Think about the terms listed in this chart. Put an X in the boxes that best describe your knowledge of each term.

	I Can Give a Definition	I Can Give an Example	I Have No Idea
mean			
median			
mode			
range			
outlier			
histogram			
box plot			
scatter plot			

Copyright © 2014 Taylor & Francis. Excerpt from *Math Lesson Starters for the Common Core, Grades 6–8: Activities Aligned to the Standards and Assessments* by Paige Graiser, Ed.D.

Dependent or Independent?

Determine if each of the following pairs of events involves dependent or independent events.

a.	Flipping a coin, then rolling a die	☐ dependent events ☐ independent events
b.	Drawing a card from a deck of 52 cards, then drawing a second card	☐ dependent events ☐ independent events
c.	Rolling a die, then rolling a second die	☐ dependent events ☐ independent events
d.	Spinning a game spinner twice	☐ dependent events ☐ independent events
e.	Taking and eating a candy from a jar that contains equal amounts of cherry and orange candies, then taking a second candy	☐ dependent events ☐ independent events

Copyright © 2014 Taylor & Francis. Excerpt from *Math Lesson Starters for the Common Core, Grades 6–8: Activities Aligned to the Standards and Assessments* by Paige Graiser, Ed.D.

Anticipating Measures of Central Tendency

Directions: Read each statement in the middle of the chart. On the left-hand side, labeled "Warm-Up," check if you agree or disagree with the statement. Leave the right-hand side, labeled "After Class," blank until your teacher instructs you to complete the assignment.

Warm-Up			After Class	
Agree	Disagree	Statement	Agree	Disagree
		The median is the middle-most value of a data set.		
		The mode is the most recurring number in a data set.		
		If the median is more than the mean, then the data set is skewed to the left.		
		If a set contains an even number of data, then the median will be equal to the mean of the two numbers in the middle of the data set.		
		The mean = median = mode of every data set.		

Copyright © 2014 Taylor & Francis. Excerpt from *Math Lesson Starters for the Common Core, Grades 6–8: Activities Aligned to the Standards and Assessments* by Paige Graiser, Ed.D.

Number Line Match-Up

Match each labeled point on the number line below with the correct measure of central tendency of this set of data:

12, 18, 11, 12, 14, 13, 11, 10, 11

_____ Mean

_____ Median

_____ Mode

_____ Range

_____ Maximum

_____ Minimum

Copyright © 2014 Taylor & Francis. Excerpt from *Math Lesson Starters for the Common Core, Grades 6–8: Activities Aligned to the Standards and Assessments* by Paige Graiser, Ed.D.

Missing Data

Octavia is working with a set of data.

$$4, 16, 4, m, 16, 16$$

If the mean of Octavia's data set is 12, how can she find the value of m? Calculate the value of m.

Copyright © 2014 Taylor & Francis. Excerpt from *Math Lesson Starters for the Common Core, Grades 6–8: Activities Aligned to the Standards and Assessments* by Paige Graiser, Ed.D.

Joshua's Homework

Joshua is having a difficult time deciding if his homework problem should be solved by using a permutation or a combination.

a. How would you explain the difference between combinations and permutations to Joshua?

b. Decide whether the question can be answered with a combination or a permutation.

c. Answer the question.

Joshua's Homework		
Problem	**Method**	**Answer**
For homework, you must answer 4 questions from a list of 12 questions. In how many ways can you complete the homework?	☐ Combination ☐ Permutation	

Copyright © 2014 Taylor & Francis. Excerpt from *Math Lesson Starters for the Common Core, Grades 6–8: Activities Aligned to the Standards and Assessments* by Paige Graiser, Ed.D.

Barney's Burger Blast advertises that they have 84 possible value-meal combinations. A value meal consists of a burger, a side dish, and a milk shake. The menu lists seven types of burgers and three side dishes. How many types of milkshakes are available on a value meal at Barney's?

Explain your answer.

Barney's Value Meals

Choose from:

7 Awesome Burgers!
3 Delicious Sides!
? Frosty Milkshakes!

84 Meal Combinations!

Copyright © 2014 Taylor & Francis. Excerpt from *Math Lesson Starters for the Common Core, Grades 6–8: Activities Aligned to the Standards and Assessments* by Paige Graiser, Ed.D.

Probability Fill-In

Many things cannot be predicted with total certainty. We can use _____ to describe how _____ something is to happen.

Probability can be expressed as a _____ or a _____.

The _____ is all the possible outcomes of an _____.

| event | ratio | chance | likely |

| sample space | percent | probability |

Copyright © 2014 Taylor & Francis. Excerpt from *Math Lesson Starters for the Common Core, Grades 6–8: Activities Aligned to the Standards and Assessments* by Paige Graiser, Ed.D.

Sample Space

When you roll a die, there are six possible outcomes in the sample space:

What happens when you roll two dice at the same time? What are the possible outcomes? Complete the possible outcomes of rolling two dice using the blank dice below.

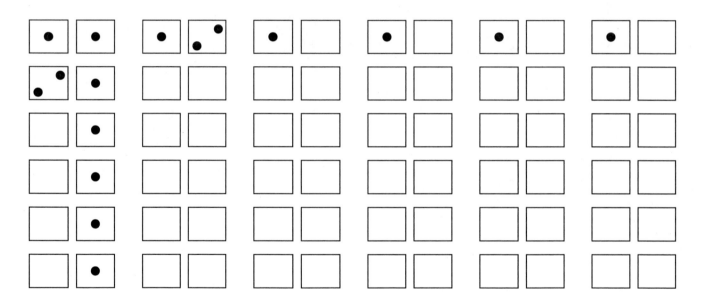

Answer the following questions using the data above:

a. How many ways can you roll a seven? _____

b. How many outcomes contain at least one six? _____

c. What is the chance of rolling a total of one? _____

Copyright © 2014 Taylor & Francis. Excerpt from *Math Lesson Starters for the Common Core, Grades 6–8: Activities Aligned to the Standards and Assessments* by Paige Graiser, Ed.D.

Samples and Surveys

Chloe made a list of sampling methods and how members are chosen:

Sampling Method	How Sample Members are Chosen
Random Sample	By chance, at random
Convenience Sample	Easiest to find
Systematic Sample	According to a set rule or formula
Voluntary Sample	Members choose to join the sample

Identify the sampling method used for each of the situations below:

A store awards coupons to every 20th person who enters the store.	The science club president draws three names from a box of all the club member's names to determine who will attend the national convention.	A teacher distributes a survey about school safety to her homeroom class.	A radio host asks listeners to call in and nominate their favorite coffee shop for a contest.
Method:	Method:	Method:	Method:

Copyright © 2014 Taylor & Francis. Excerpt from *Math Lesson Starters for the Common Core, Grades 6–8: Activities Aligned to the Standards and Assessments* by Paige Graiser, Ed.D.

Sports Cards

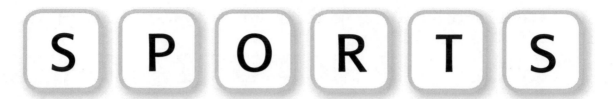

Jon says the probability of drawing an S out of the above card set at random is $\frac{1}{6}$.

Do you agree with Jon? Is there something that Jon is not taking into consideration?

Explain.

Copyright © 2014 Taylor & Francis. Excerpt from *Math Lesson Starters for the Common Core, Grades 6–8: Activities Aligned to the Standards and Assessments* by Paige Graiser, Ed.D.

Mental Math: Probability

Calculate the following using only your mind—*no calculators, no paper, no pencils.*

- Start with the number of sides on a die.
- Multiply by the probability of drawing a heart at random from this set of cards:

- Multiply by the probability of a coin landing on "heads."
- Subtract the probability of drawing a red marble out of a bag that has 12 red marbles and 16 blue marbles.
- What is your answer?

Copyright © 2014 Taylor & Francis. Excerpt from *Math Lesson Starters for the Common Core, Grades 6–8: Activities Aligned to the Standards and Assessments* by Paige Graiser, Ed.D.

Sometimes, Always, or Never: Probability

Determine if the following statements are sometimes true, always true, or never true. Please explain your choice.

If you roll a die 100 times, you will roll the same number of 2s and 5s.	☐ Sometimes True ☐ Always True ☐ Never True	Why:
In a school, there will be two people who share the same birthday.	☐ Sometimes True ☐ Always True ☐ Never True	Why:

Copyright © 2014 Taylor & Francis. Excerpt from *Math Lesson Starters for the Common Core, Grades 6–8: Activities Aligned to the Standards and Assessments* by Paige Graiser, Ed.D.

Scatter Plots

 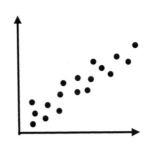

Mandy knows that scatter plots can show a positive correlation, a negative correlation, or no correlation.

a. Label the type of correlation found in the scatter plots above.

Positive? Negative? Neither?

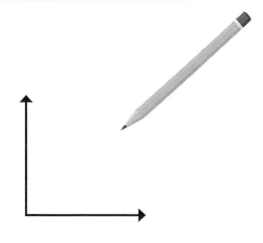

b. Draw a scatter plot that shows no correlation.

Copyright © 2014 Taylor & Francis. Excerpt from *Math Lesson Starters for the Common Core, Grades 6–8: Activities Aligned to the Standards and Assessments* by Paige Graiser, Ed.D.

Unit Reflection
Statistics & Probability

What worked well:

_____

_____

_____

_____

_____

What I would do differently:

_____

_____

_____

_____

_____

My next steps:

_____

_____

_____

_____

_____

UNIT 6
Lesson Starters to Use with Multiple Math Topics

In most sciences one generation tears down what another has built, and what one has established, another undoes. In Mathematics alone each generation adds a new storey to the old structure.

Hermann Hankel

Writing in Mathematics

Writing in mathematics is an essential tool for students to process what they know and have recently learned. It is also an essential tool for teachers to assess their students' knowledge and gain insight into student understanding.

At the beginning of the school year, writing prompts are also an excellent way for math teachers to get to know their students and assess their preferred methods of learning. The following sentence stems make great Lesson Starters for the beginning of the school year.

- My all-time favorite math activity was _____ because . . .
- My worst experience in a math class was . . .
- My three goals for this semester/school year are . . .
- I want to increase my understanding of math so that I can . . .
- When I read a word problem, the first thing I do is . . .
- The thing I liked the most about last year's math class was . . .
- The thing I liked the least about last year's math class was . . .
- My favorite math teacher was _____ because . . .

Copyright © 2014 Taylor & Francis. Excerpt from *Math Lesson Starters for the Common Core, Grades 6–8: Activities Aligned to the Standards and Assessments* by Paige Graiser, Ed.D.

Student Behavior Reflection: Substitute Teacher

When a teacher is absent, she is often unsure of what she will be facing when she returns to the classroom. This student behavior scale allows students to reflect upon their own behavior and rate their productivity while their classroom teacher was away. This is a great way to start the class following a teacher's absence.

CATEGORY	4	3	2	1
Assignment	I stayed focused on my assignment throughout the class period, and I completed all work assigned.	I stayed focused on my assignment throughout most of the class period. I am almost finished with my assignment.	I was not very focused on my work, or I was completing work for another class. I have completed half of my assignment.	I did not focus on my work, and I have completed less than half of my assignment.
Behavior	I never had to be reprimanded by the substitute, and I was helpful.	I had to be reminded once to be helpful and behave well by the substitute teacher.	I had to be reminded two or three times to behave well.	I had to be removed from the classroom.

My Score: $\dfrac{\square}{8} = $ _____ %

My Comments:

Copyright © 2014 Taylor & Francis. Excerpt from *Math Lesson Starters for the Common Core, Grades 6–8: Activities Aligned to the Standards and Assessments* by Paige Graiser, Ed.D.

Word Association Vocabulary Cards

Mathematical vocabulary practice is a great topic for Lesson Starters.
Word Association cards are a great strategy because they reach
a variety of learning styles. For a Lesson Starter, have students
complete one or two index cards.

Front of Card   Back of Card

term	illustration
ray	
definition	**personal association**
A ray is a part of a line that begins at one point and extends in one direction without stopping.	*A sun ray extends forever through space.*

Teaching Tip

Punch a hole in the top left of each index card so students
can use binder rings, brads, or even yarn to keep their cards
together.

Copyright © 2014 Taylor & Francis. Excerpt from *Math Lesson Starters for the Common Core, Grades 6–8: Activities Aligned to the Standards and Assessments* by Paige Graiser, Ed.D.

Carroll Diagrams

A Carroll Diagram or Lewis Carroll Square is named after the pseudonym of Charles Dodgson, author of *Alice's Adventures in Wonderland*. Dodgson was also a well-known math lecturer and math textbook writer.

Carroll Diagrams are used for grouping things and can be applied to a variety of mathematical topics.

Example:

	Even	Odd
Prime	2	3, 5, 7, 11, 13, 17, 19, 23
Not Prime	4, 6, 8, 10, 12, 14, 16, 18, 20, 22, 24	1, 9, 15, 21, 25

Try these for Lesson Starters:

	Numbers that are multiples of 6	Numbers that are not multiples of 6
Numbers that are multiples of 9		
Numbers that are not multiples of 9		

	Regular Polygons	Not Regular Polygons
Quadrilaterals		
Not Quadrilaterals		

Copyright © 2014 Taylor & Francis. Excerpt from *Math Lesson Starters for the Common Core, Grades 6–8: Activities Aligned to the Standards and Assessments* by Paige Graiser, Ed.D.

Alphabet Boxes

Alphabet Boxes is a useful strategy for having students review their notes from previous lessons. Students flip through their notes and categorize information on the unit by letter of the alphabet. For example, the Pythagorean Theorem would be placed to fill the box that contains the letter P. This can be made more challenging by assigning fewer letters to each box.

A, B, C	D, E, F	G, H, I	J, K, L
M, N, O	**P, Q, R**	**S, T, U, V**	**W, X, Y, Z**

Copyright © 2014 Taylor & Francis. Excerpt from *Math Lesson Starters for the Common Core, Grades 6–8: Activities Aligned to the Standards and Assessments* by Paige Graiser, Ed.D.

Review/Preview

Just as the name implies, in this Lesson Starter students review what they learned in the previous day's (or week's) lesson and then predict what they will study next.

A	List three things we learned in yesterday's lesson.		
B	Predict what we will study next.		

Copyright © 2014 Taylor & Francis. Excerpt from *Math Lesson Starters for the Common Core, Grades 6–8: Activities Aligned to the Standards and Assessments* by Paige Graiser, Ed.D.

Complete List of Lesson Starters

Lesson Title	I've Tried This ✓
Ratios and Proportional Relationships	
Rate Your Knowledge: Proportional Relationships	
Ratios and Roses	
Delores's Ratio Practice	
The Sweet Shop	
Concrete Proportions	
Interest Fill-In	
Temperature Change	
Function Fun	
A Taxing Phone Problem	
Number Line Story Time	
Rearranging Interest	
Model House	
The Number System	
Anticipating Adding and Subtracting Integers	
Rational and Irrational Number Sort	
Fractions and Decimals	
Jumpstart: Integers	
Anticipating Division of Rational Numbers	
Ordering Rational Numbers	
Fractions, Decimals, and Percents	
Write about It: Reasonable Answers	
Sometimes, Always, or Never: Adding and Multiplying	

Graphing Irrational Numbers	
A Negative Discussion	
Absolute Value Homework	
Mental Math: Number Sense	
Decimal Expansion: What's Missing?	
LCM and GCF Fill-In	
Finding Factors of Monomials	
Write a Like Term	
Expressions & Equations	
Equation Selection	
Jumpstart: Variables	
Expression Match-Up	
What's the Difference?	
Equation Fill-In	
Write about It: Calculating Steps	
What Am I?	
The Power of Parentheses	
Mental Math: Linear Equations	
Reciprocal Riddle	
Inequality Flip?	
Scientific Notation Reports	
Order Matters	
Anticipating Linear Equations in Two Variables	
Applying Slope	
Geometry	
Describe the Difference	
Analogies: Geometry Terms	

Do You Know Your Geometry Symbols?	
Sometimes, Always, or Never: Polygons	
Pythagoras's Candy Shop	
Triangle Sketching I: Sides	
Triangle Sketching II: Angles	
Feature Analysis: Polygons	
Shape-Shifting Matrix	
Mental Math: Geometry	
Circle Fill-In	
Angle-*ing*	
Line-Up	
Write about It: Area and Perimeter	
Volume of Cubes	
Rate Your Knowledge: Angle Relationships	
Anticipating Angles	
Statistics & Probability	
Rate Your Knowledge: Statistics	
Dependent or Independent?	
Anticipating Measures of Central Tendency	
Number Line Match-Up	
Missing Data	
Joshua's Homework	
Barney's Burger Blast	
Probability Fill-In	
Sample Space	
Samples and Surveys	
Sports Cards	

Mental Math: Probability	
Sometimes, Always, or Never: Probability	
Scatter Plots	
Lesson Starters to Use with Multiple Math Topics	
Writing in Mathematics	
Student Behavior Reflection: Substitute Teacher	
Word Association Vocabulary Cards	
Carroll Diagrams	
Alphabet Boxes	
Review/Preview	

Selected Answers

1. Ratios & Proportional Relationships

Ratios and Roses: Yes, this scenario can be modeled by both Jorge's and Joel's ratios and their calculated costs (unit rates). It is important that students realize that it is not the context that determines the order of the quantities; the order is dependent on what we want to know.

Delores's Ratio Practice: yes; no (Delores did not completely reduce the fraction); no (ratios are not expressed as mixed numbers); no (Delores appears to have solved the problem correctly but mistakenly rounded up her answer).

The Sweet Shop: The answer is C. To calculate Courtney's total cost, you have to calculate the cost of the individual item (unit rate).

Concrete Proportions: Batch 1 = 4; Batch 2 = 33, 22; Batch 3 = 27, 9.

Temperature Change: Lauren's proportion is incorrect.

Function Fun: yes; yes; no; no.

A Taxing Phone Problem: Tabatha is incorrect. She calculated the tax on both the phone and the connection fee.

Model House: The model house will be 54 inches tall.

2. The Number System

Rational and Irrational Number Sort: Gordon's error was in categorizing $\sqrt{9}$ as an irrational number. The $\sqrt{9}$ can be simplified to 3, which can be written as a fraction (3/1).

Fractions and Decimals

Fraction	Decimal Expansion	Does the Decimal Repeat or Terminate?
1/3	$0.\overline{3}$	Repeats
1/20	0.05	Terminates
1/11	0.09	Repeats
1/5	0.2	Terminates
1/9	$0.\overline{1}$	Repeats
1/10	0.1	Terminates

Jumpstart: Integers:

	Add	Subtract	Multiply	Divide
3, 2	$3 + 2$ 5	$3 - 2$ 3	$3 \cdot 2$ 6	$3 \div 2$ 3/2
4, 4	8	0	16	1
$-4, (-4)$	-8	0	16	1
$-4, 4$	0	-16	-8	-1
$4, -4$	0	8	-16	-1

Ordering Rational Numbers: a. correct; b. incorrect (it is possible that Lorenzo assumed that since $7 > 5$, then -7 would also be greater than -5); c. correct; d. correct; e. incorrect (Lorenzo may be assuming that any number is greater than zero).

Graphing Irrational Numbers: The $\sqrt{3}$ would be plotted between 1.7 and 1.8. The $\sqrt{6}$ would be plotted between 2.4 and 2.5.

A Negative Discussion: Elizabeth is correct.

Absolute Value Homework: correct; incorrect; correct; incorrect; incorrect.

Mental Math: Number Sense: 4.

Decimal Expansion: What's Missing?: 10; 8; 1/100; 2; 1/10,000.

3. Expressions & Equations

Equation Selection: One possible question for William might be: *Is the teacher asking you to subtract the value of x from 10 or is she asking you to subtract 10 from the value of x?*

Jumpstart: Variables

	Add	Subtract	Multiply	Divide
x, y	$x + y$	$x - y$	xy	x/y
$-x, -y$	$-x + (-y)$	$-x + y$	xy	x/y
$x, -y$	$-x + (-y)$	$x + y$	$-xy$	$-x/y$
x, x	$2x$	0	x^2	1

Expression Match-Up: Many students will insist that they have an extra expression. Ask students if their extra expression has anything in common with any of the other expressions. Question students about the expressions $2(x + 2)$ and $2x + 4$. Do they have anything in common?

What's the Difference?: a. 80,000; 8. b. >. c. 8.0×10^4; 8.0.

The Power of Parentheses: a. answers will vary; b. no; c. answers will vary.

Mental Math: Linear Equations: -3.

Reciprocal Riddle: You end up with your original number.

Inequality Flip?: no; yes; yes; yes.

Scientific Notation Reports: 2.0×10^{29}; 7.5×10^{-4}.

Applying Slope: 1/3; -3; -3.

4. Geometry

Analogies: Geometry Terms: perimeter; compass; rotation; line; cylinder.

Pythagoras's Candy Shop: It does not matter if the students choose the one large candy bar or the two smaller bars. According to the Pythagorean Theorem, both quantities are the same.

Triangle Sketching I: Sides: equilateral; isosceles; scalene.

Triangle Sketching II: Angles: acute; obtuse; right.

Mental Math: Geometry: 26.

Angle-*ing*: acute; obtuse; obtuse; straight; obtuse; acute.

Volume of Cubes: c.

5. Statistics & Probability

Dependent or Independent?: independent; dependent; independent; independent; dependent.

Number Line Match-Up: mean, e; median, d; mode, c; range, b; maximum, f; minimum, a.

Missing Data: $m = 16$.

Joshua's Homework: permutation.

Barney's Burger Blast: There are 4 milkshake flavors.

Samples and Surveys: systematic; random; convenience; voluntary.

Sports Cards: Jon is incorrect. The probability is 1/3 (reduced from 2/6). He did not include the second S.

Mental Math: Probability: 3/7.

Index

absolute value 29, 31, 42, 43
acute triangle 82, 87
angles 73, 77–8, 87, 92
anticipation guide 31, 35, 67, 92, 102
arc 77
arca 73, 89
assessment 1

behavior 2–3, 118
box plot 100

Carroll Diagram 120
center 86
chance 107
circle 76–7, 86
circumference 77, 86
combinations 105–6
Commutative Property 66
complementary angles 91
compass 77
composite 45
cone 74
correlation 113
corresponding anglcs 91
cube 77, 90
cylinder 74, 77

decimal 33, 37
decimal expansion 29, 33, 44
denominator 35
dependent events 101
diameter 86
diamond 76
domain 29
double number line 11, 23

equation 29, 51, 54, 58, 60, 68
equilateral triangle 81, 84
event 107
exponent 42–3
expression 29, 51, 54, 58, 60–1

factorization 45–6
formula 20, 51, 58, 60, 73
fraction 16, 29, 33, 37, 41
function 12, 21, 52

googol 44
graphing 34, 41
greatest common factor 45

histogram 100

independent events 100
inequality 36, 42, 57, 54
integer 29, 31, 34, 41
interest 19, 24
interior angles 91
irrational numbers 29, 32, 40
isosceles triangle 81

knowledge rating 14, 91, 100

least common multiple 45
like term 46
linear equation 12, 52, 62, 67
line 67, 77
line segment 78
lines of symmetry 79
lowest terms 16

Printed by PGSTL